A TEEN GUIDE *to* *Fast, Delicious* LUNCHES

CONTENT ADVISER: Joan Bushman, RD, MPH,
Dietician and Wellness Specialist

READING ADVISER: Alexa L. Sandmann, EdD,
Professor of Literacy, College and Graduate School of
Education, Health, and Human Services,
Kent State University

COMPASS POINT BOOKS
a capstone imprint

Compass Point Books
151 Good Counsel Drive
P.O. Box 669
Mankato, MN 56002-0669

Editor: Jennifer Fretland VanVoorst
Designers: Veronica Correia and Heidi Thompson
Media Researcher: Wanda Winch
Food Stylist: Sarah Schuette
Library Consultant: Kathleen Baxter
Production Specialist: Sarah Bennett

Image Credits
Alamy: Jeff Morgan 05, 4–5; ArtParts Stock Illustrations, illustrations of food and kitchen objects throughout book; Capstone
Studio: Karon Dubke, cover (top all), 13 (all), 15, 17, 19, 21, 23, 25 (all), 27, 29, 31, 33, 35, 39, 41, 43, 44 (all), 47, 49, 51, 53;
Dana Meachen Rau, 64 (middle), iStockphoto: Alija, 8, fatihhoca, 45, Kati Molin, cover (bottom left), Kim Gunkel, 60, Steve
Debenport, 57; Shutterstock: Anton Albert, cover (bottom middle left), 9, AVAVA, 59 (left), Christopher Halloran, 24–25,
D. Copy, back cover, Elena Elisseeva, 1, Elena Schweitzer, 54 (top), fantasista, 62, Gleb Semenjuk, cover background, Ian
O'Hanlon, 100% stamp used throughout book, icyimage, cover (bottom middle right), Maksim Shmeljov, 58–59 (bottom),
62–63 (bottom), 64 (bottom), Monkey Business Images, 12, Morten Heiselberg, 63, Stephen Coburn, 6–7, Thaiview, 10–11
(background), wacpan, cover (bottom right), Yuri Arcurs, 36–37, ZanyZeus, 59 (right).

Library of Congress Cataloging-in-Publication Data
Rau, Dana Meachen, 1971–
  A Teen guide to fast, delicious lunches / by Dana Meachen Rau.
   p. cm. — (Teen cookbooks)
  title: Fast, delicious lunches
  Includes index.
  Summary: "Information and recipes help readers create
quick, healthy, and tasty lunches"—Provided by publisher.
  ISBN 978-0-7565-4405-8 (library binding)
  1. Luncheons—Juvenile literature. 2. Cookbooks. I. Title.
II. Title: Fast, delicious lunches.
  TX735.R37 2011
  641.5'3—dc22   2010040680

Visit Compass Point Books on the Internet at *www.capstonepub.com*

Printed in the United States of America in North Mankato, Minnesota.

092010   005933CGS11

TABLE OF CONTENTS

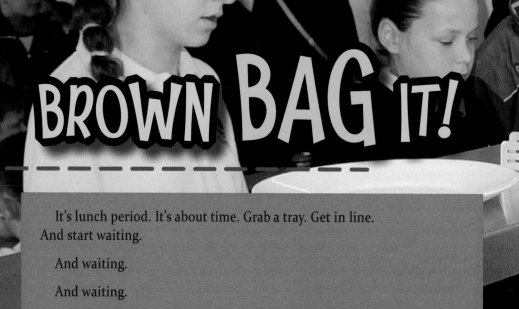

BROWN BAG IT!

It's lunch period. It's about time. Grab a tray. Get in line. And start waiting.

And waiting.

And waiting.

Lunch period is really short. You need time to eat, check in with your friends, and relax for a minute. But instead you're still waiting.

And waiting ...

Finally you reach the counter. Lumpy chicken? Or limp noodles? Let's face it: The school cafeteria isn't a five-star restaurant. Aren't those beans supposed to be green? Oh well. At least there's pudding.

No sooner have you found a seat than ...

RING! It's the bell. Lunch is over. The lunch monitor tells you to get moving.

"But the pudding ..." you say.

"No time for pudding!" she barks.

Lunch period goes by fast. You can't always count on the cafeteria, but you can bring your own lunch. It doesn't have to be a flattened peanut butter and jelly sandwich, bruised apple, and stale pretzels. Make an awesome brown bag lunch to satisfy your midday appetite. With a few extra minutes on a school morning, you can pull together a portable feast.

Of course, not all lunches have to be on the go. On a day off or weekend, sit down to a nice meal at home. Invite friends over, crank up the music, and make lunch together. You can even host a lunch-making party. Try making a few different recipes, divide them into servings, pack them up, and send everyone home with containers. You'll all have a stock of fast and delicious brown bag lunches. And you'll always have time for pudding.

Less in The Landfill

It's better to "brown bag it" without a brown bag! Try packing your lunch in a reusable lunch bag. Instead of plastic baggies to hold your sandwiches, use a reusable sealed container. Bring drinks in reusable bottles too.

Sure, it's nice when your parents buy the groceries, make you lunch, and clean up afterward. But the downside is that you don't get to pick what you want or prepare it the way you like. Why not have the best lunch you can have? Why not make it yourself?

The first step on the path to lunch nirvana is the grocery store. Write out a list, and head down those aisles.

Produce

If you can only remember one rule when shopping, remember this one: Fresh is best! The produce aisle can be overwhelming with all the colorful piles of fruits and vegetables. Look for ones that are firm and bright, not limp, mushy, or bruised. If you buy fruits a few days before you plan to use them, they will ripen more at home. Vegetables need to be used within a few days to keep their freshness. You can get most fruits and vegetables any time of year, because growers fly and truck produce all over the country and the world. But it's better to buy fruits and vegetables that are in season where you live. Grocery stores sometimes buy their produce from local farms. At a farmers market, you can buy your fruits and vegetables right from the grower too. You can also visit a roadside stand or pick-your-own farm—or even grow your own garden. Then you'll know your food is fresh.

Refrigerated Foods

Some foods spoil. You can't buy a gallon of milk and wait three weeks to drink it. It'll taste nasty and may make you sick. Meat, poultry, fish, eggs, and all dairy foods are kept in refrigerators in the grocery store to stay fresh longer. The manufacturers even tell you how long before they'll spoil. Notice the "sell by" or "use by" dates on their packages. After this date, you run the risk of eating unsafe food.

Packaged Foods

Look for dates on packaged foods too. Boxes of crackers, cans of beans, and jars of peanut butter won't spoil for a long time, but they will lose their freshness and might turn unpleasant after a while. So look for "best if used by" dates on the packages to see when to eat them. Also read the nutritional labels on the packages. They list the ingredients, the amounts of fats, sugars, protein, and carbohydrates in the food, and all the other information you need to make the best food choices.

Organics

Organic foods are a healthful option. These foods are grown, raised, or processed on farms that use methods of farming that are less harmful to the environment. Organic farmers fight weeds and other crop pests with natural methods instead of chemicals. They do not inject antibiotics or hormones into their livestock. Instead they raise their crops and livestock in more natural conditions to keep them—and you—healthy.

HOW TO AVOID ...

... UpseTTing The Grownups.

Don't give your parents another reason to take away your game system or ground you from a slumber party. Instead butter them up for times you need them—like when you need money for a field trip or when you want to stay up late on a school night. Keep the kitchen clean when you cook. They'll love that.

Sometimes when you're creative in the kitchen, things can get messy. Keep it under control by tidying up as you go. After you're done with a utensil, toss it in the sink. Put ingredients away as you use them. Wipe up any spills on the floor so you don't slip. Then when you're done making your meal, cleanup will be a whole lot easier.

... Burning The House Down.

Many house fires start in the kitchen. If a towel gets too close to a hot burner, it can ignite. So push up your sleeves, tie your apron, and keep towels or any other fabric away from the burners on your stove.

Fires can also be caused by overheating oil in pan. Never leave oil heating alone. Keep a fire extinguisher in the kitchen. Water doesn't put out this type of fire—it only makes it worse.

... A Trip To The Emergency Room.

Be cautious when you cut. Knives are better when they're sharp—they are less likely to slip off the food and cut your finger instead. But a sharp knife can do some major damage to your finger. Always cut away from you, and focus on what you're cutting, not other distractions in the kitchen.

The stove and oven are hot spots for burns. Pots can be easily knocked off the stove top if the handles are sticking out, so keep handles pointed in. Steam from a pot can burn your face, so don't stick your nose too close. Wear oven mitts when taking anything in and out of the oven.

Keep the area around electrical appliances dry. Don't stretch cords over an area where someone could trip on them and send your appliances soaring off the counter. Unplug appliances when you're done with them.

... Seeing Your Lunch Come Back Again.

Germs are lurking in many corners of the kitchen. You don't want bacteria getting in your food, because it can make you sick—and that's not very appetizing. Keep meats, poultry, fish, eggs, dairy foods, and most fruits and veggies in the refrigerator. The low temperatures in there slow the growth of bacteria. Look for the "sell by" or "use by" dates on their packages. If a date has passed, don't eat the food. If something smells funny or looks odd, don't eat it either. Making sure such foods as meat, poultry, and eggs are thoroughly cooked is a must for killing bacteria too.

If your brown-bag lunch uses ingredients from the fridge, you'll have to keep them cold until lunchtime. Pack a freezer pack with your lunch to keep your food cool until you eat it.

And keep it clean. Wash your hands well with warm water and soap before you cook. Wash fruits and vegetables with gently running cold water too. You want to remove any lingering bacteria from yourself and your foods so they don't end up in your meal. After you cook, wash your hands again. Clean all the dishes you used in hot, soapy water—or even better, in the dishwasher. Clean up the counters too. A good lunch isn't just delicious or healthful. It's safe too!

HOW TO USE THIS BOOK

Each fast, delicious recipe is divided into three parts. Food Stuff lists all the ingredients you need. Kitchen Gear lists the equipment you'll need. Prep Steps are the step-by-step instructions to follow to make your meal.

Make sure to check out the number of servings of each recipe. Some are lunches for one. Others feed more. Adjust the ingredients (halve or double the recipe) as you need to.

Sometimes you might come across a kitchen tool or technique you're not familiar with. How can you use a microwave to melt something if you don't know what the terms mean? Many of these cooking terms are defined in the back of the book. Look them up in either the Tools Glossary (page 56) or the Technique Glossary (page 58).

Conversion Charts

WEIGHT	UNITED STATES	METRIC
	1 ounce	30 grams
	½ pound	225 g
	1 pound	455 g

TEMPERATURE	DEGREES FAHRENHEIT	DEGREES CELSIUS
	250°F	120°C
	300°F	150°C
	350°F	180°C
	375°F	190°C
	400°F	200°C
	425°F	220°C

Look for special stamps on some recipes:

Some recipes can be made more portable to bring to school. The *Brown Bag It* stamp offers suggestions for sizing and packing your lunch to go.

Check out the *If You're a Vegetarian* stamp. Here you'll find foods to replace the nonvegetarian items in the Food Stuff lists.

Even if you're not a vegetarian, you still may want to change a recipe. Look for the *Call in the Subs* stamp to learn about alternative ingredients.

VOLUME	UNITED STATES	METRIC
	¼ teaspoon	1 milliliter
	½ teaspoon	2.5 mL
	1 teaspoon	5 mL
	1 tablespoon	15 mL
	¼ cup	60 mL
	⅓ cup	80 mL
	½ cup	120 mL
	1 cup	250 mL
	1 quart	1 liter

NO NEED TO WAIT IN THAT LONG CAFETERIA LINE ANYMORE. AND NO NEED TO WAIT TO GET COOKING!

WHICH SANDWICH?

Putting together a sandwich isn't rocket science. But a sandwich is more than just bread, stuff, bread. A sandwich can be a unique creation that reflects your personality. Are you sweet and gooey like peanut butter and jelly? Are you clean and crisp like lettuce on toast?

Perhaps you're spicy?

Meaty?   Cheesy?

Which sandwich are you?

ZOMBIE CHICKEN SALAD PITA

You thought you'd finished the chicken for dinner last night. But it wasn't gone for good. It's back the next day, like a zombie returning to take revenge.

Turn leftover chicken into something you can eat for lunch—before it eats you!

Food Stuff

1 cup cooked chicken, cut into small pieces

1 stalk celery—about ¼ cup chopped

8-10 red seedless grapes

1½ tablespoons nonfat plain yogurt

¼ teaspoon curry powder

2 tablespoons slivered almonds

1 piece whole wheat pita bread

Kitchen Gear

Dry measuring cups

Measuring spoons

Knife

Medium mixing bowl

Small mixing bowl

Spoon

Makes one sandwich

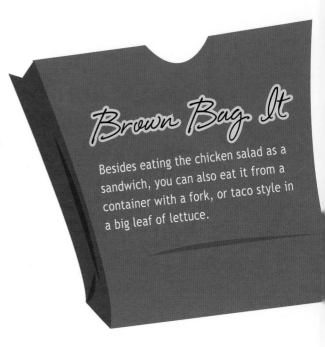

Brown Bag It

Besides eating the chicken salad as a sandwich, you can also eat it from a container with a fork, or taco style in a big leaf of lettuce.

Prep Steps

1. Place the cooked chicken pieces in a medium bowl.

2. Chop the stalk of celery. Cut the grapes into quarters. Add both to the bowl with chicken.

3. In a separate, small bowl, stir together the yogurt and curry powder. Add to the chicken mixture.

4. Sprinkle on the almonds and mix all the ingredients together.

5. Spoon the chicken salad into the pita.

No Go, Mayo

Mayonnaise is used in sandwiches to add a tangy flavor. But it is made from oil, egg yolks, and vinegar all whipped up together. It adds a lot of fat to a dish. Using nonfat yogurt in this recipe instead of mayonnaise keeps the tang but cuts the fat.

Quick-cook Chicken

If you don't have chicken leftovers to haunt you the next day, you can still make this recipe. To cook a chicken breast, heat water in a saucepan until it's boiling. Add a boneless chicken breast, cover, and boil for about 12 to 15 minutes or until the chicken is no longer pink inside.

Call in the Subs

You can replace the red grapes with raisins or dried cranberries. Both will give you a sweet flavor.

COLD PIZZA SANDWICH

Sure, pizza is delicious hot and stringy right out of the box. But cold pizza is a taste sensation too. Make this quick pizza fresh from the fridge.

Food Stuff

1 grinder, sub, or hoagie roll

Extra-virgin olive oil

3 ounces fresh mozzarella

5 strips roasted red peppers

3 slices tomato

2 fresh basil leaves

Salt and pepper

Kitchen Gear

Knife

Pastry brush

Makes one sandwich

Prep Steps

1. Cut the roll in half lengthwise and open. Brush the insides of both halves with olive oil.

2. Slice the mozzarella. Lay the slices on one half of the bread. Add salt and pepper to taste.

3. Lay the peppers, tomato, and basil leaves on top of the mozzarella.

4. Top it with the other half of the roll.

Fresh Mozzarella

You can usually find fresh mozzarella in the deli section of your grocery store. It's often kept in water to keep it moist. It also comes in various sizes. The little ones are best tossed in salads. The larger ones are better for slicing and adding to sandwiches.

Brown Bag It

You can avoid a soggy roll by bringing the mozzarella, tomato, and red peppers in a separate, sealed container. At home brush the bread with olive oil, sprinkle with salt and pepper, and put in the basil. At school insert the other ingredients.

Call in the Subs

You can add other pizza ingredients to this sandwich too. Olives, pepperoni, artichokes, and sun-dried tomatoes make this cool sandwich even cooler!

POWER-UP PEANUT BUTTER

Peanut butter and jelly are always partners, but frankly, PB has had just about enough of J. It's been itching to branch out and try something new. You can too with these new partners for peanut butter.

Food Stuff

2 slices whole grain bread

2 tablespoons peanut butter

2 teaspoons sunflower seeds

1 tablespoon dried fruit

½ of one banana

Kitchen Gear

Measuring spoons

Spreader

Knife

Makes one sandwich

Prep Steps

1. Spread both slices of bread with peanut butter.

2. On one slice of bread, sprinkle the sunflower seeds and dried fruit.

3. Cut the banana into small slices, either coins or lengthwise strips. Lay them on the sandwich.

4. Top it off with the other slice of bread.

Brown Bag It

Since nothing in this sandwich can spoil (at least not before lunch), you don't even need a freezer pack!

Call in the Subs

If you're allergic to peanut butter, you may be able to use other "butters" made from nuts or seeds. How about almond butter, cashew butter, or sunflower seed butter? But check with a parent or guardian before you try any substitutions in case peanuts aren't your only allergy. And always check labels well to be sure a product is completely peanut-free.

Just as there are many types of jelly that taste good with peanut butter, you can also use many kinds of dried fruit for this recipe. Raisins and dried cranberries are great additions. Try dried cherries, blueberries, or apricots too.

Maybe you're not into thick, bulky sandwiches that you can hardly fit your mouth around. Maybe you like things small and simple. Make a mini sandwich with two crackers and a sweet and salty spread in between. You can eat it in one bite. (You'll probably want more than one to satisfy your appetite at lunchtime!)

Food Stuff

10 whole wheat crackers

5 teaspoons goat cheese

5 teaspoons raspberry preserves

Kitchen Gear

Measuring spoons

Spreader

Makes five cracker sandwiches

Prep Steps

1. Spread 1 teaspoon of goat cheese and 1 teaspoon of raspberry preserves on a cracker. Repeat on four more crackers.

2. Put the remaining five cracker lids on top of the cheese and preserves.

Not Just for Cows

Most cheese is made from cow's milk. But goats make milk too. Goat cheese has a tangy taste unlike other cheeses. It comes in logs and containers. Some goat cheeses are drier and better for crumbling on salads. For this recipe, look for goat cheese that is easily spreadable.

Call in the Subs

Any type of jelly, jam, or preserves will work for this recipe. You can also replace the goat cheese with cream cheese.

NEW SPIN PINWHEEL CLUB

Club sandwiches are usually tall towers of turkey, bacon, lettuce, tomato, and toast. But why settle for the usual? Put a unique spin on a club sandwich with a swirl of flavors rolled into a tortilla.

Join the club! It's so delicious it will make you dizzy!

Food Stuff

2 tablespoons light cream cheese

2 teaspoons sliced green onions

1 whole wheat tortilla

2 ounces honey turkey

2 slices turkey bacon

1 leaf romaine lettuce

3 slices tomato

Kitchen Gear

Measuring spoons

Small mixing bowl

Spreader

Plate

Paper towels

Makes one sandwich

Prep Steps

1. Cook the bacon according to package directions. Drain any extra fat on paper towels. Set aside.

2. In a small bowl, combine the cream cheese and onions. Mix together with the spreader.

3. Lay the tortilla flat on a plate. Spread the cream cheese mixture all over the tortilla.

4. Lay the slices of turkey on top of the cream cheese.

5. Lay the bacon on top of the turkey, close to one end of the tortilla. Keep all the ingredients as flat as possible.

6. Place the lettuce and tomato on top of the bacon.

7. To roll your tortilla, start at the end with the bacon. Roll the ingredients into the tortilla until you get to the end. "Glue" the end closed with the cream cheese.

Call in the Subs

If you're a vegetarian, try filling this pinwheel with a variety of vegetables instead of the turkey and bacon. Bean sprouts, peppers, and cucumbers put a new spin on this club sandwich too.

Brown Bag It

Wrap this sandwich tightly in paper or plastic wrap so it stays closed until you're ready to break it out for lunch.

Bail on The Bacon

When you cook regular bacon, you can see the glistening fat oozing out of it as you fry it. Turkey bacon is a good substitute. It has a lot less fat and fewer calories than regular bacon.

HOT SPOTS

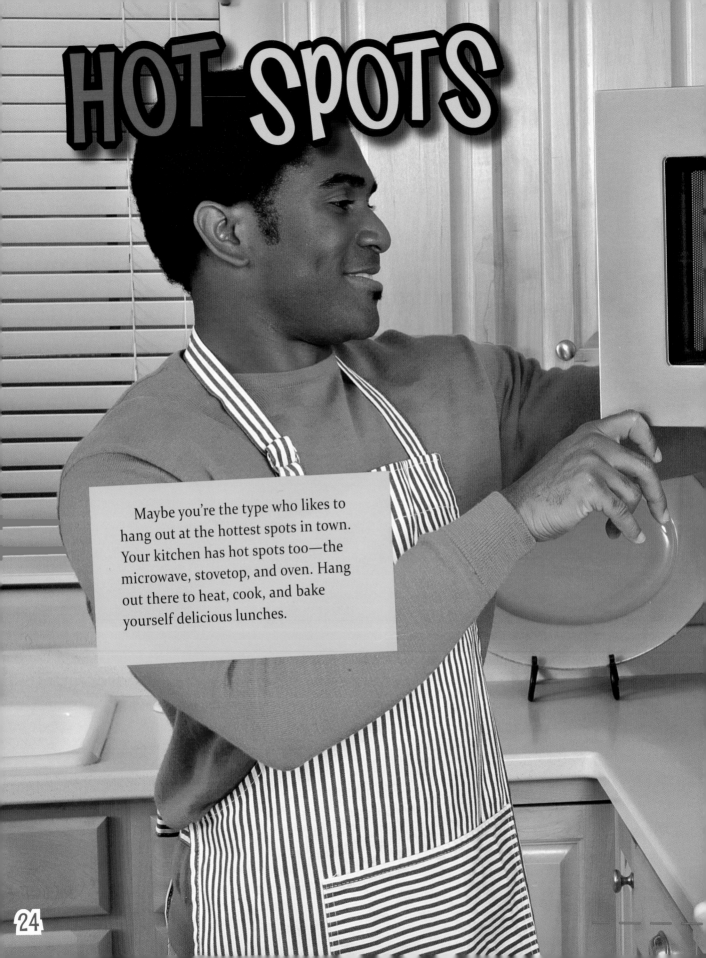

Maybe you're the type who likes to hang out at the hottest spots in town. Your kitchen has hot spots too—the microwave, stovetop, and oven. Hang out there to heat, cook, and bake yourself delicious lunches.

BROC AND CHEESE BREADSTICKS

You tap drumsticks on your drum set, knee, door frame, or chair to keep to the beat of the music. Keep a healthier rhythm with veggie sticks oozing with cheese.

Food Stuff

1 cup chopped frozen broccoli
¾ cup whole wheat flour
1 cup white flour
½ cup skim milk
1 tablespoon butter, softened
1 teaspoon baking powder
⅔ cup grated cheddar cheese
Vegetable cooking spray
Salt and pepper
Skim milk

Makes 12 breadsticks

Kitchen Gear

Dry measuring cups
Liquid measuring cup
Measuring spoons
Colander
Knife
Mixing bowl
Spatula
Baking sheet
Small bowl
Pastry brush
Turner
Wire cooking rack

Brown Bag It

Wrap up a few sticks for a portable lunch you can even eat walking between classes!

Prep Steps

1. Preheat the oven to 400°F.

2. Cook the broccoli according to the package directions. Drain well in a colander. Cut the cooked broccoli into tiny pieces. Set aside.

3. In a mixing bowl, combine the flours, milk, butter, and baking powder. Add in the broccoli and the cheese. Stir with a spatula (or with your hands) until the ingredients form a ball of dough.

4. Place the dough on a flat surface sprinkled with flour. Knead the dough about five times.

5. Divide the dough into 12 balls of the same size.

6. Spray the baking sheet with cooking spray.

7. Roll each ball of dough in your palms or on the floured surface to form a stick about 6 to 8 inches (15 to 20 centimeters) long. Lay the sticks on the baking sheet.

8. Pour a little milk in a small bowl and brush on the tops of the sticks with a pastry brush. Sprinkle with salt and pepper.

9. Bake the sticks at 400°F for about 18 to 20 minutes or until browned and crispy. With a turner, move the sticks to a wire rack to cool.

Tips for Measuring Flour

Flour needs to be light and airy to get an accurate measurement. If you need a cup of flour, don't dip the whole measuring cup into your flour bag. The flour will be too tightly packed inside. Instead spoon the flour into the cup a little at a time. Level off the top with the straight side of a table knife so it is completely flat and level with the brim. Then you'll have the right amount.

Spray Oil vs. Butter

Vegetable cooking spray is oil in an aerosol container. It keeps food from sticking to pans when you cook. You can also use butter or margarine. But spray oil helps you use less fat. If you would rather use butter, use a small amount—just enough to coat the bottom of the pan or baking sheet

You're never too old for chicken nuggets. They're tasty hot or cold, and with a choice of sauces, you can dip your way to many flavor combinations.

Food Stuff

1 pound boneless and skinless chicken breasts

2 large eggs

2 tablespoons milk

⅓ cup white flour

⅔ cup plain bread crumbs

Vegetable cooking spray

Barbecue sauce

Makes four to six servings

Kitchen Gear

Dry measuring cups

Measuring spoons

Baking sheet

Knife

Shallow bowl

Whisk

2 plates

Turner

Brown Bag It

Since this chicken tastes good cold too, wrap up a few pieces to bring to school. Keep your dipping sauce in a small, airtight container.

Prep Steps

1. Preheat the oven to 400°F.

2. Spray the baking sheet with vegetable cooking spray.

3. Cut the chicken into 4- to 5-inch (10- to 13-cm) long thin strips. Set aside.

4. Break the eggs into a shallow bowl. Add the milk. Beat together with a whisk.

5. Pour the flour onto one plate. Pour the bread crumbs onto another.

6. Take a chicken strip and roll it in the flour until well covered. Then dip it into the egg mixture until it is well covered. Finally, roll the chicken strip in the bread crumbs so it is fully coated. Place it on the baking sheet.

7. Repeat with the rest of your chicken strips: flour first, egg second, and bread crumbs third.

8. Spray all of the breaded chicken on the baking sheet with cooking spray.

9. Bake in the oven at 400°F for seven minutes. Flip the chicken over with a turner, and bake for another five minutes or until the center is no longer pink and the bread crumbs have lightly browned.

10. Serve with barbecue sauce for dipping.

Better Baked

The chicken fingers or nuggets you get at fast food restaurants are often fried in fatty oils. By baking these chicken sticks instead of frying them, you cut out a lot of the fat.

Call in the Subs

You can try variations on this basic recipe. Instead of plain bread crumbs and barbecue sauce, experiment with other varieties:

Italian: Italian seasoned bread crumbs; tomato sauce for dipping

Asian: Panko bread crumbs; duck sauce for dipping

Mexican: Cornmeal; salsa for dipping

Buffalo: Plain bread crumbs mixed with hot pepper sauce; blue cheese dressing for dipping

MONSTER MUENSTER GRILLED CHEESE

Move over, American! There's a new cheese in town. Meet Muenster. He sounds like a monster, though he's really quite mild. But mix in some spicy jalapeños, and now he's got the teeth to give your meal a real bite.

Food Stuff

2 tablespoons raspberry preserves

1 tablespoon coarse ground mustard

1 or 2 jalapeño slices

Butter

3 slices Muenster cheese (about 2 ounces)

2 slices whole grain bread

Kitchen Gear

Measuring spoons

Blender

Spreader

Medium skillet

Turner

Knife

Makes one sandwich and ¼ cup of sauce

Prep Steps

1. In a blender, combine the preserves, mustard, and jalapeño slices. Blend together into a sauce.

2. Spread a little butter on both slices of bread. Put one piece of bread in the skillet, butter side down. Lay on the slices of cheese, and place the other piece of bread on top, butter side up.

3. Heat the skillet on medium. After about two minutes, flip the sandwich with a turner. Cook on the other side for another minute or until the bread is golden and toasted.

4. Remove the grilled cheese sandwich from the skillet with the turner. Cut in half. Dip the sandwich in the sauce to eat.

Not the Dipping Type?

Spread the sauce onto the inside of the bread before grilling instead of keeping it separate.

Call in the Subs

Substitute any type of cheese for the Muenster—American, cheddar, and Monterey Jack cheeses all melt well.

BUSTED SWEET POTATO

Hey! Someone broke my sweet potato! Try this mash up of sweet flavors for a filling lunch.

Food Stuff

1 small sweet potato

2 teaspoons butter

2 teaspoons maple syrup

⅛ teaspoon cinnamon

1 tablespoon chopped pecans

Kitchen Gear

Measuring spoons

Vegetable brush

Fork

Microwave

Knife

Spoon

Makes one serving

Prep Steps

1. Scrub the potato with the vegetable brush under cool running water to clean off any dirt. Dry the potato and poke it about 10 times with a fork.

2. Place the potato in the microwave. Cook on high for about five minutes, or until a knife slides easily into the potato.

3. Cut a slit from end to end on one side of the potato. Push in on the ends. The potato will open like a little bowl.

4. Put the butter on the potato while the potato is still hot. With a spoon, loosen up the inside of the potato and stir it around within the skin until the butter melts.

5. Add the syrup, cinnamon, and pecans. Stir so the ingredients are well combined.

Potato Explosion

Why do you need to stab the skin of the potato with a fork before you microwave it? If you don't, steam will build up inside the potato and it might explode all over the inside of your microwave!

The Skinny on the Skin

You can eat the skin of a sweet potato, as long you scrub it well before you cook it. The skin is full of nutrients and fiber. Your body needs fiber to keep things moving through your digestive system.

Call in the Subs

You can use a regular potato as easily as a sweet one. Follow the directions on the opposite page to cook your white potato in the microwave. Instead of the sweet taste of syrup, cinnamon, and pecans, stir in 1 tablespoon of light cream cheese, chopped chives, and a little garlic salt.

LUCKY LEFTOVER FRIED RICE

If you're lucky, when you open the fridge, you'll find a bunch of leftovers that you can combine into a quick lunch. Fried rice is a perfect way to use up leftover rice and cooked veggies from the previous night's dinner. Add some tofu, and you'll have a good dose of protein too.

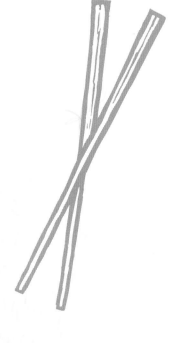

Food Stuff

2 ounces firm tofu

1 teaspoon peanut oil

½ cup cooked vegetables

¼ teaspoon dried onion flakes

1 cup cooked brown rice

2 tablespoons soy sauce

⅛ teaspoon dry ground ginger

½ teaspoon honey

Green onion, sliced

Kitchen Gear

Measuring spoons

Dry measuring cups

Medium skillet

Wooden spoon

Knife

Makes two servings

Call in the Subs

All kinds of vegetables—peas, carrots, green beans, lima beans, corn, broccoli, red peppers, green peppers, snow pea pods, or asparagus—would be tasty in this recipe. If you don't have leftover cooked veggies, frozen mixed vegetables make this recipe really quick too. You don't even have to cook them first. Just thaw them before you put them in the skillet.

If you don't want to venture into tofu-land, you can use precooked ham, bacon, pork, or chicken as the protein in this recipe too.

Prep Steps

1. Cut the tofu into small cubes.

2. Prepare the skillet by adding 1 teaspoon peanut oil and heating the pan on medium to medium high. Add the tofu.

3. Cook and stir the tofu with a wooden spoon for about two minutes. While the tofu continues cooking, add the vegetables and onion flakes. Cook and stir the tofu and vegetables for another two to three minutes or until the tofu is lightly browned.

4. Add the cooked rice, soy sauce, ginger, and honey. Fry the rice for a few minutes until it gets slightly crispy. Stir to combine.

TOFU, Who?

Never met tofu before? Tofu is made from soybeans and has the texture of soft cheese. It is a pretty bland food, but it absorbs whatever flavors it's cooked with. Get to know tofu. It's full of protein, low in fat, and a great source of calcium.

THE COOL FACTOR

What does it take to have the cool factor?

Be cool by being different. Try these unique lunches that can be eaten cold. Before you know it, everyone else will want to try these cool lunches too.

CHILLY CHILI

At chili festivals, chefs spend hours sweating over hot, steaming pots, hoping their chili is voted the winner. There's a faster, easier way to get a blast of spicy chili flavor without spending hours in the kitchen—or even having to cook at all!

Food Stuff

1 cup canned kidney beans

1 cup canned black beans

1 cup canned diced tomatoes

½ cup sliced pitted black olives

2 tablespoon sliced green onions

2 teaspoons diced jalapeño peppers

½ teaspoon dried oregano

1 teaspoon chili powder

¼ teaspoon dried cumin

Hot sauce

Grated cheddar cheese

Kitchen Gear

Dry measuring cups

Measuring spoons

Colander

Bowl

Spoon

Makes four servings

Prep Steps

1. Drain the kidney beans, black beans, and canned tomatoes in a colander and rinse them with cold water. Place in a bowl.

2. Add the olives, green onions, peppers, oregano, chili powder, and cumin. Stir well to combine all the ingredients.

3. Taste it. If you would like it spicier, add some drops of hot sauce to taste, or add more diced jalapeños.

4. Sprinkle with grated cheddar cheese when serving.

Dip It

Having friends over and out of salsa? Make a bowl of chilly chili and scoop it up with corn tortilla chips.

PEANUT BUTTER NOODLES

Expand your worldview to the east and break away from the usual pasta and red sauce. Thai chefs mix interesting flavors, such as peanuts, coconut, and hot peppers, to create unique noodle dishes.

Food Stuff

Handful of dry spaghetti, about 1 inch (2.5 cm) in diameter

2 tablespoons creamy peanut butter

2 teaspoons unsweetened light coconut milk

1 tablespoon water

2 teaspoons soy sauce

½ teaspoon lime juice

¹/₁₆ teaspoon dry grated ginger

1 teaspoon sesame seeds

Dash of cayenne pepper

Kitchen Gear

2-quart saucepan

Colander

Mixing bowl

Whisk

2 forks

Makes two servings

Prep Steps

1. In a saucepan boil the spaghetti according to package directions. Drain in a colander. Or use leftover cold spaghetti (without sauce).

2. In a mixing bowl, add all of the other ingredients. Whisk together until smooth.

3. Add the cooked spaghetti to the mixture. Toss with two forks until well coated with sauce.

Brown Bag It

Make this meal "to go" by packing it in a container. Bring along a fork or chopsticks.

GASP! GAZPACHO

Soup sounds like a good lunch choice on a cold winter day. But (gasp!) it's sometimes too hot during the rest of the year to eat soup for lunch. Never fear. Gazpacho is a cold soup. On a hot day, you'll wish you had a bowl of gazpacho big enough to swim in.

Food Stuff

1 tomato, chopped—about 1 cup

½ cup chopped red pepper

1 small cucumber, peeled and chopped—about 1 cup

½ cup tomato juice

1 teaspoon lemon juice

1 teaspoon olive oil

⅛ teaspoon garlic powder

⅛ teaspoon dried cilantro

⅛ teaspoon salt

⅛ teaspoon pepper

Sliced green onions

Kitchen Gear

Dry measuring cups

Liquid measuring cup

Measuring spoons

Vegetable peeler

Knife

Blender

Makes two 1-cup servings

Prep Steps

1. Peel the skin off of the cucumber. Chop the tomato, red pepper, and cucumber into chunks. Put into the blender.

2. Pour in the tomato juice, lemon juice, and olive oil. Add the garlic powder, salt, and pepper.

3. Puree the ingredients together.

4. Garnish each serving with sliced green onions.

Brown Bag It

Bring gazpacho in your lunch bag sealed in an insulated container made to hold liquids so it doesn't leak.

Call in the Subs

If you like your food spicy-hot, add sliced jalapeños before you puree the ingredients, or add hot sauce after.

Soak It Up

After you're done with a hot day of soaking up the rays, soak up this soup with Italian or French bread, or cut cubes of the bread to float on top.

SIDEKICKS

Everyone needs a trusty sidekick—a friend to watch your back, offer advice, and tell you when you've got food in your teeth.

Round out your lunch with a sidekick too.

CUCUMBER COMBO

Salad doesn't have to have lettuce. Cucumbers can be the base for a colorful salad that combines snappy flavors to create a tangy bite.

Food Stuff

2 cups chopped cucumber

¼ cup chopped red onion

¼ cup sliced black olives

⅓ cup feta cheese, crumbled

4 teaspoons olive oil

1 teaspoon balsamic vinegar

¼ teaspoon dried oregano

Kitchen Gear

Dry measuring cups

Measuring spoons

Vegetable peeler

Bowl

Knife

Whisk

Makes two to three servings

Prep Steps

1. Peel the cucumber with a vegetable peeler. Cut into small pieces. Place in a bowl.

2. Add the chopped onion and sliced olives to the bowl with the cucumber. Add the feta cheese.

3. In a separate bowl, combine the olive oil and vinegar. Whisk together until the liquids are no longer clear.

4. Pour over the cucumber mixture. Sprinkle on oregano and stir gently.

Brown Bag It

It's easy to pack this salad for lunch. Just bring along a fork. The longer it sits, the stronger the flavor.

Call in the Subs

You can dice two tomatoes to add to this salad too.

RABBIT FOOD RAW SLAW

Rabbits are smart. They know that veggies are most healthful when they're eaten right from the garden. You may not want to crouch in the garden and eat the way rabbits do. Cut the veggies up instead and eat them alongside your lunch.

Food Stuff

1 cup shredded green cabbage

½ cup shredded red cabbage

½ cup shredded carrots

1 stalk celery

1 tablespoon vegetable oil

1 teaspoon lemon juice

1½ teaspoons honey

⅛ teaspoon dried ginger

Kitchen Gear

Dry measuring cups

Measuring spoons

Mixing bowls

Knife

Whisk

Makes one serving

Prep Steps

1. Combine the shredded cabbages and carrots in a mixing bowl. Chop the celery stalk and add to the bowl.

2. In a separate small bowl, add the vegetable oil, lemon juice, honey, and ginger. Whisk together. Pour over the cabbage and toss until coated.

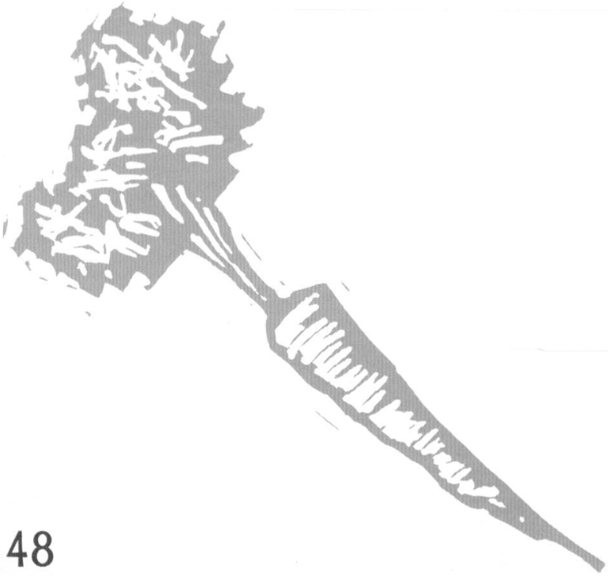

Make It a Meal

You can promote this slaw from side dish to main meal by stirring in a small can of tuna and sprinkling it with crumbled bacon.

The Work's All Done!

You can buy preshredded cabbage and carrots in the produce section of many grocery stores.

OMG! AMBROSIA

According to ancient myth, if you eat ambrosia—the food of Greek and Roman gods—you'll become immortal. So why not whip up a batch? Even if it doesn't work, it will taste good trying!

Food Stuff

1 6-ounce container nonfat vanilla yogurt

½ teaspoon orange zest

½ cup canned pineapple chunks

½ cup canned pear slices

½ navel orange

3 tablespoons flaked coconut

Mini marshmallows

Kitchen Gear

Dry measuring cups

Measuring spoons

Mixing bowl

Zester

Colander

Knife

Spoon

Makes 1½ cups

Prep Steps

1. Empty the container of yogurt into a mixing bowl.

2. Place the orange zest in the bowl with the yogurt. Stir well.

3. In a colander, drain the canned pineapple and canned pears. Add to the bowl.

4. Cut the peel off the orange with a knife. Cut the orange into pieces. Place in the bowl.

5. Add the coconut. Stir everything well.

6. Garnish each serving of ambrosia with five to six marshmallows.

Get to the Good Stuff

Need a quick way to get past the thick peel and right to the juicy orange flesh of an orange? First cut the orange in half. Then slice off the rounded top. From the top, slice down along the sides to remove the peel.

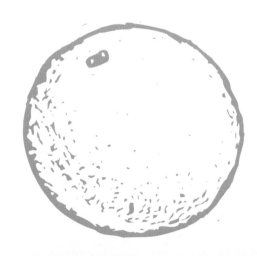

Call in the Subs

Try other flavors of yogurt and other fruits for new creamy combinations.

BUMPY PRETZEL PUDDING

It's been a bumpy road all morning. Your bus was late. Your locker was stuck. You tripped in the hallway. You've been waiting long enough for this sweet midday boost. Sit back, relax, and enjoy a well-deserved dessert.

Food Stuff

1 4-ounce package instant chocolate pudding

2 cups milk

½ cup crumbled pretzels

¼ cup mini peanut butter or butterscotch chips

½ cup slivered almonds

½ cup mini marshmallows

Kitchen Gear

Liquid measuring cup

Dry measuring cups

Mixing bowl

Whisk

Spatula

Four bowls

Plastic wrap

Makes four servings

Prep Steps

1. Prepare pudding according to package directions, mixing 2 cups of milk with the pudding mix. Whisk for two minutes.

2. Stir in the pretzel pieces, peanut butter or butterscotch chips, almonds, and marshmallows gently with a spatula.

3. Pour the pudding into four bowls. Cover each with plastic wrap. Place in the refrigerator. Keep chilled until ready to eat.

Brown Bag It

No more waiting in the cafeteria line! By bringing it with you, there's always time for pudding.

CHEW ON THIS!

Lunch falls right in the middle of your busy day. Half the day is done, another half to go! Whether you like a hot lunch or bag lunch, soup or a sandwich, a nibble or a chomp, what you eat can give you enough energy to get through the afternoon.

It's simple. Your body needs food to function. The more healthy the food, the better your body works—and the better you'll feel. So know what you eat.

CARBOHYDRATES

You're an active, energetic person. Where does all that energy come from? Sugar. Yes, sugar. Carbohydrates are the sugars found in food that your body converts into energy. But not all sugars are created equal. Whole grains, fruits, and vegetables will give your body the energy it needs to run strong all day long.

Grains: Do you make your sandwich from white or whole wheat bread? Both are made from grains, and both have carbohydrates. But whole wheat bread is better for you. Whole grain foods still contain a lot of their original nutrients. Refined grains, like white bread, have been made white by taking out a lot of healthful stuff. Wheat, corn, rice, and oats are all good whole grains to make a part of your daily diet.

Fruits and vegetables: When it comes to fruits and veggies, you have lots of choices for lunch. Portable ones, like apples, grapes, bananas, carrot sticks, and celery sticks are easy to pack in your lunch bag.

Avoid foods with added sugar. The natural sugars in foods are often as much sweetness as you need. The wrong kinds of sugars can make you feel full. Then you won't have room left for healthful foods.

PROTEIN

Protein is a power food. It builds up your muscles, strengthens your bones, and helps all of your body systems. It's easy to make protein a part of your lunch.

Meat, beans, and eggs: These foods all have a good dose of protein. Avoid processed lunch meat. Instead try eggs, which are quick and easy to cook. Beans are great in salads. Or try the soybean product tofu, which can replace meat in many meals.

Nuts: There are so many nuts to choose from: peanuts, almonds, cashews, walnuts, pistachios, and more! Delicious in all kinds of dishes, nuts add crunchy bits of protein.

Dairy products: Drink a big glass of milk, eat a container of yogurt, or nibble on some cheese. All of these dairy foods contain protein and calcium. Nonfat or low-fat dairy foods contain less fat than regular dairy foods and are a better way to add dairy protein to your diet.

If you treat your body well, it will treat you well too.

FAT AND SALT

Your body needs both fat and salt. Fat stores the energy your body needs. Salt helps balance your body's fluids. But people often eat too much fat and salt. Many foods, especially processed ones, contain extra fat and salt to enhance their flavor. You can enhance flavor in your lunches by adding healthful ingredients instead.

Try to get your fats from natural sources, like nuts, vegetables such as olives and avocados, and plant oils such as olive oil and sunflower oil. Try to avoid solid fats such as butter, shortening, and animal fat.

Remember the phrase you learned in elementary school, "You are what you eat"? Please. When you eat a banana, you don't turn into one. But your body does use all the food it takes in. So why not give it what it wants and needs? If you treat your body well, it will treat you well too.

TOOLS GLOSSARY

Baking sheet
flat metal pan used to bake cookies and other baked goods

Blender
appliance with a rotating blade that mixes solids and liquids together

Colander
bowl dotted with holes to drain liquids from foods

Dry measuring cups
containers the size of specific standard measurements. Dry cups come in ¼ cup, ⅓ cup, ½ cup, and 1 cup sizes. Measure dry ingredients over an empty bowl, not over your mixture, in case of spills. Level off dry ingredients with a table knife.

Liquid measuring cup
a container marked at intervals along the sides to accurately measure amounts of liquid. A liquid measuring cup is usually marked at ¼ cup, ⅓ cup, ½ cup, ⅔ cup, ¾ cup, and 1 cup intervals. Hold the cup at eye level to check the measurement.

Measuring spoons
spoons the size of specific standard measurements. Measuring spoons come in ¼ teaspoon, ½ teaspoon, 1 teaspoon, and 1 tablespoon measurements. There are 3 teaspoons in a tablespoon.

Microwave
appliance that cooks food with radio waves. Make sure the cup, bowl, or plate you use is microwave-safe. Microwaving heats food and the container it's in, so use oven mitts to remove it from the microwave.

Pastry brush
small brush used to apply liquids on top of foods

Saucepan
round deep metal pan with a handle and a lid, used on a stovetop

Skillet
round, shallow metal pan with a handle, used on a stovetop

Spatula
flat tool used to mix ingredients or scrape the side of a bowl

Spreader
tool used to put a thin layer of a soft food onto another food

Turner
flat tool used to flip foods from one side to the other or to remove foods from a pan

Vegetable brush
stiff brush used to clean the dirt off vegetables

Vegetable peeler
tool that separates the peel or skin of a fruit or vegetable from its flesh

Whisk
tool made of looped metal wires used to add air into a mixture by beating it rapidly

Wire cooling rack
rack made of a grid of metal wires that allows air to reach the top, bottom, and sides of food to cool it quickly

Zester
tool used to remove a thin layer of peel or skin

TECHNIQUE GLOSSARY

Beat

stir very quickly to help add air to a mixture

Boil

heat until small bubbles form on the top of a liquid

Dice

cut into very small pieces

Dough

mixture that becomes stiff enough to form with your hands

Drain

remove liquid by pouring it off or placing it in a colander

Fry

cook something on a stovetop in hot fat

Garnish

decorate

Grate

cut into thin strips by rubbing against a grater

Knead

mix dough in a way to work the glutens (a type of protein found in flour). To knead dough, you flatten the dough with the heel of your hand, fold the dough in half, and press down again.

Melt

heat a food to turn it from solid to liquid

Peel

take off the outer covering of a fruit or vegetable

Preheat

turn the oven on ahead of time so it is at the correct temperature when you are ready to begin baking

Puree
blend a food until it is smooth

Shred
cut into small thin strips, often with a grater

Slice
cut into thin pieces with a knife

Spread
put a thin layer of a soft food onto another food

Thaw
bring frozen food to room temperature

Toss
mix by lifting ingredients in an up and down motion

"To Taste"
to your liking. Recipes often leave the amount of seasoning ingredients up to the cook, so you can add more or less, depending on what you like.

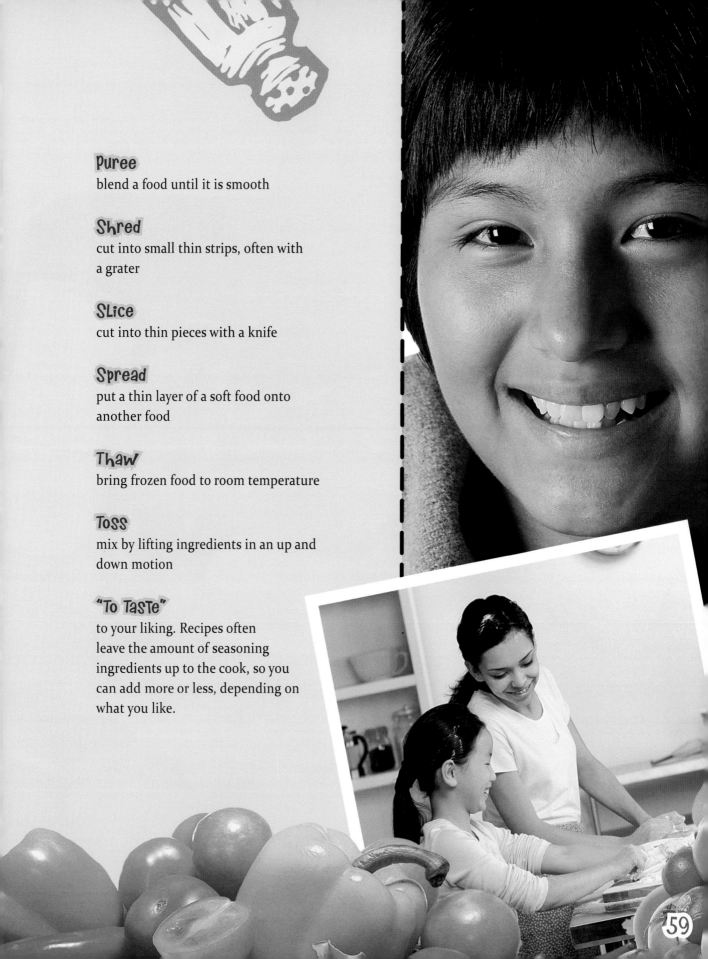

READ MORE

Carle, Megan, and Jill Carle. *Teens Cook: How to Cook What You Want to Eat.* Berkeley, Calif.: Ten Speed Press, 2004.

Dunnington, Rose. *Super Sandwiches: Wrap 'em, Stack 'em, Stuff 'em.* New York: Lark Books, 2006.

Gold, Rozanne. *Eat Fresh Food: Awesome Recipes for Teen Chefs.* New York: Bloomsbury USA, 2009.

Stern, Sam, and Susan Stern. *Cooking Up a Storm: The Teen Survival Cookbook.* Cambridge, Mass.: Candlewick Press, 2005.

INTERNET SITES

Use FactHound to find Internet sites related to this book. All of the sites on FactHound have been researched by our staff.

Here's all you do:
Visit *www.facthound.com*
Type in this code: 9780756544058

ACKNOWLEDGEMENTS

Many thanks to friends and family members who sampled my creations and shared recipe advice. I am grateful to Paula Meachen, Patricia Rau, Denise Genest, and the Tuesday morning writers. Additional thanks to the teens of my neighborhood who e-mailed me lists of their favorite foods. An extra nod to Chris, Charlie, and Allison, who ate and drank the good and the bad and never held back their honest opinions.

Dana Meachen Rau

INDEX

ABOUT THE AUTHOR

Dana Meachen Rau

Dana Meachen Rau is the author of more than 250 books for children, from preschoolers to teens. She loves baking cookies, shopping at local farms, and growing tomatoes and basil in her backyard garden. Her favorite food by far is chocolate. Even in summer, she usually enjoys a steaming cup of hot cocoa every day.